William Shakespeare's

Twelfth Night

or

'What You Will'

EDITED BY

Philip Page and Marilyn Pettit

ILLUSTRATED BY

Philip Page

Published in association with

The
Basic Skills
Agency

Hodder & Stoughton

A MEMBER OF THE HODDER HEADLINE GROUP

Orders: please contact Bookpoint Ltd, 39 Milton Park, Abingdon, Oxon OX14 4TD.
Telephone: (44) 01235 400414, Fax: (44) 01235 400454. Lines are open from 9.00–6.00,
Monday to Saturday, with a 24 hour message answering service.
Email address: orders@bookpoint.co.uk

British Library Cataloguing in Publication Data
A catalogue record for this title is available from The British Library

ISBN 0 340 74295 X

First published 1999
Impression number   10 9 8 7 6 5 4 3 2
Year   2005 2004 2003 2002 2001 2000 1999

Text Copyright © 1999 Phil Page and Marilyn Pettit
Illustrations Copyright © 1999 by Phil Page

Cover illustrations by Lee Stinton
Typeset by Fakenham Photosetting Ltd, Fakenham, Norfolk
Printed in Great Britain for Hodder & Stoughton Educational, a division of Hodder
Headline Plc, 338 Euston Road, London NW1 3BH by J. W. Arrowsmith Ltd., Bristol.

Contents

About the play

Twelfth Night is one of Shakespeare's comedies. Comedies are supposed to make you laugh.

Did you notice the words '*supposed to*'? Sometimes, words and actions that some people find funny, other people find silly and boring, especially when the words were written hundreds of years ago! So perhaps you won't laugh much – at first.

But remember, when you read this play, that Shakespeare had to follow the rules of comedy.

However many bad things happen in the play, he has to make sure that everything will end happily. His comedies usually end with a wedding and a party.

To make us laugh, he has disguises, plenty of mistakes that lead to very funny problems, lots of music, dancing, joking, even a clown.

Read on . . . and see if you can work out what some of the rules of comedy are.

Cast of characters

Viola
She pretends to be a man called **Cesario** when she works for Orsino.

Sebastian
Viola's twin brother.

Antonio
A sea-captain. Sebastian's friend and Orsino's enemy.

Orsino

Duke of Illyria. A fair and generous man.

Olivia

A Countess, kind and virtuous. In mourning for her dead brother.

Sir Toby Belch

Olivia's relative. A drunkard who enjoys having a good time and playing tricks on people.

Sir Andrew Aguecheek

Sir Toby's cowardly and rather stupid friend.

Maria

Olivia's maid. A lively and fun-loving young woman.

Malvolio

Olivia's steward. A miserable, big-headed man.

Clown

Olivia's jester.

Fabian

Olivia's servant.

| Act 1 Scene 1 | Orsino is in love with Olivia. He wants to know how she feels about him. His messenger tells him she is mourning for her dead brother. She will not think of love for seven years. |

> If music be the food of love, play on,
> Give me excess of it, that, **surfeiting**,
> The appetite may sicken, and so die.

> O, when mine eyes did see Olivia first,
> Methought she **purg'd the air of pestilence**.

> How now! What news from her?

> I might not be admitted,
> But from her handmaid do return this answer:
> **The element itself**, till seven years' heat,
> Shall not behold her face at ample view.

surfeiting – having too much
purg'd the air of pestilence – made the air sweeter
The element itself – the air

Viola has been saved from a shipwreck. She thinks that her twin brother has been drowned. The ship's captain says there is a chance he is still alive.

What country, friends, is this?

This is **Illyria**, lady.

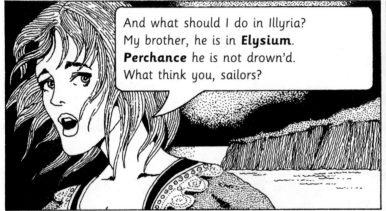

And what should I do in Illyria? My brother, he is in **Elysium**. **Perchance** he is not drown'd. What think you, sailors?

It is perchance that you yourself were saved.

O, my poor brother! and so perchance may he be.

True, madam, and to comfort you with chance, I saw your brother bind himself to a strong mast that liv'd upon the sea.

Illyria – what used to be Yugoslavia
Perchance – by chance/with luck

Elysium – heaven

The captain tells Viola about Orsino and how he is in love with Olivia. Viola comes up with a plan. She will disguise herself as a man and work for Orsino.

Who governs here?

Orsino.

Orsino . . . I have heard my father name him.
He was a bachelor then.

And so is now, or was so, very late;
For but a month ago I went from hence,
And then **'twas fresh in murmur**
That he did seek the love of fair Olivia.

What's she?

A virtuous maid, the daughter of a count that died leaving her in the protection of her brother, who also died.

Conceal me what I am, I'll serve this Duke.

Think about it

Why is it important in this comedy to use the word 'perchance' and for the captain to say that he saw Viola's brother 'bind himself to a strong mast'?

What might these words be preparing us for later in the play?

'twas fresh in murmur – it was rumoured
Conceal me what I am – Don't tell anybody that I'm a woman

| Act 1 Scene 3 | Maria tells Sir Toby off. They talk about Sir Toby's friend, Sir Andrew Aguecheek. |

Sir Toby: What a plague means my niece to take the death of her brother thus? I am sure care's an enemy to life.

Maria: By my troth, Sir Toby, you must come in earlier o' nights: your cousin, my lady, takes great exceptions to your ill hours.

Sir Toby: Why, let her except, before excepted.

Sir Toby decides that Olivia can think what she likes!

Maria: Ay, but you must confine yourself within the modest limits of order.

Sir Toby: Confine? I'll confine myself no finer than I am. These clothes are good enough to drink in, and so be these boots too; and they be not, let them hang themselves in their own straps.

Sir Toby disagrees with Maria and uses the word 'confine' to mean 'dress up'.

Maria: That quaffing and drinking will undo you. I heard my lady talk of it yesterday, and of a foolish knight that you brought in one night here, to be her wooer.

Sir Toby: Who? Sir Andrew Aguecheek?

Maria: Ay, he.

Sir Toby: He's as **tall** a man as any's in Illyria.

Maria: What's that to th' purpose?

Sir Toby uses 'tall' to mean 'brave' but Maria doesn't follow. She thinks it means of great height.

Sir Toby: Why, he has three thousand ducats a year.

Maria: Ay, but he'll have but a year in all those ducats. He's a very fool and a prodigal.

Sir Andrew will soon waste all of that money.

Sir Toby: Fie, that you'll say so. He plays o' th' **viol-de-gamboys**, and speaks three or four languages word for word without book, and hath all the good gifts of nature.

A musical instrument, held between the legs.

4

Maria: He hath indeed all, most natural; for besides that he's a fool, he's a great quarreller; and but that he hath the gift of a coward to allay the **gust** he hath in quarrelling, 'tis thought among the prudent he would quickly have the gift of a grave.

gust – gift

Sir Toby: By this hand, they are scoundrels and substractors that say so of him. Who are they?

Maria: They that add, moreover, he's drunk nightly in your company.

Sir Toby: With drinking healths to my niece. I'll drink to her as long as there is a passage in my throat, and drink in Illyria: he's a coward and a coistrel that will not drink to my niece till his brains turn o' the to', like a parish top. What wench! *Castiliano vulgo* – for here comes Sir Andrew Agueface!

Sir Toby could be calling for wine or saying, 'Talk of the Devil.'

Think about it

What does this part tell you of the characters Maria and Sir Andrew?

What clues can you find that tell you that Sir Toby likes a joke and a good time?

What do you think Sir Toby is trying to do by the way he talks about Sir Andrew?

Act 1 Scene 3 Sir Andrew Aguecheek arrives and annoys Maria. He does not think he stands a chance of getting Olivia to marry him.

How now, Sir Toby Belch?

Bless you, fair **shrew**.

Accost, Sir Andrew, accost.

What's that?

My niece's chambermaid.

Good Mistress Accost, **I desire better acquaintance**.

My name is Mary, sir.

Good Mistress Mary Accost –

You mistake, knight. 'Accost' is front her, board her, woo her, assail her.

Fare you well, gentlemen.

shrew – a bad-tempered woman
I desire better acquaintance – I'd like to know you better

Accost – speak to her politely

I'll home tomorrow, Sir Toby: your niece will not be seen, or if she be, it's four to one she'll none of me: the Count himself, here hard by, woos her.

She'll none o' the Count.

Tut, **there's life in't**, man.

I'll stay a month longer.

Shall we set about some **revels**?

What shall we do else?

Let me see thee **caper**. Ha! higher! Ha! ha! excellent!

there's life in't – don't give up hope
revels – fun   **caper** – dance

Act 1 Scene 4	Viola is working for Count Orsino. She is disguised as a man and calls herself Cesario. Orsino tells Cesario (Viola) to go to see Olivia.

Orsino: Cesario,
Thou know'st no less but all. I have unclasp'd
To thee the book even of my secret soul.
Therefore, good youth, **address thy gait unto her,**
Be not denied access; stand at her doors,
And tell them, there thy fixed foot shall grow
Till thou have audience.

Orsino tells Cesario (Viola) to go to Olivia's house and not leave until he has seen her.

Viola: Sure, my noble lord,
If she be so abandon'd to her sorrow
As it is spoke, she never will admit me.

Orsino: Be clamorous, and leap all civil bounds
Rather than make unprofited return.

Orsino tells Cesario (Viola) not to bother with good manners.

Viola: Say I do speak with her, my lord, what then?

Orsino: O, then unfold the passion of my love.
Surprise her with discourse of my dear faith.
It shall become thee well to act my woes;
She will attend it better in thy youth,
Than in a **nuncio**'s of more grave aspect.

nuncio – messenger

Viola: I think not so, my lord.

Orsino: Dear lad, believe it.
For they shall yet belie thy happy years,
That say thou art a man. Diana's lip
Is not more smooth and rubious. Thy small pipe
Is as the maiden's organ, shrill and sound,
And all is semblative a woman's part.
I know thy constellation is right apt
For this affair. Some four or five attend him –
All, if you will; for I myself am best
When least in company. Prosper well in this,
And thou shalt live as freely as thy lord,
To call his fortunes thine.

Orsino is telling Cesario (Viola) how young he looks and sounds.

Viola: I'll do my best
To woo your lady. [*Aside*] Yet, **a barful strife**!
Whoe'er I woo, myself would be his wife.

a barful strife – a hard job

Think about it

What clue is there that Orsino really trusts Cesario? Do you think this might give us a clue about some thing else that might happen later on in the play between Orsino and Cesario? (Remember that Cesario is really Viola!)

How does Orsino want Cesario to act if he speaks to Olivia?

What makes us smile when Orsino describes Cesario's looks?

Cesario is going to try really hard to make Olivia return Orsino's love, but is there a clue in the aside (words that only the audience can hear) about the way Cesario feels towards Orsino?

Maria tells the Clown off for staying away from the house. The Clown tries to cheer Olivia up by making fun of her.

My lady will hang thee for thy absence.

Let her hang me.

Yet you will be hanged for being so long absent, or to be **turned away**.

Many a good hanging prevents a bad marriage.

Peace, you rogue, no more o' that. Here comes my lady.

Take the Fool away.

The lady bade take away the Fool; therefore I say take her away. Good **madonna**, give me leave to prove you a fool.

Can you do it? Make your proof.

turned away – given the sack
madonna – my lady

taste with a distempered appetite – nothing ever pleases you

Act 1 Scene 5

Cesario (Viola) arrives with Orsino's message. At first, Olivia will not see him. Then she changes her mind.

Madam, there is at the gate a young gentleman much desires to speak with you.

From the Count Orsino, is it?

I know not, madam. 'Tis a fair young man.

Who of my people hold him in delay?

Sir Toby, madam, your kinsman.

Go you, Malvolio. If it be a suit from the Count, I am sick or not at home.

Malvolio goes to see what Cesario (Viola) wants. He comes back to say that Cesario will not go away until he has seen Olivia.

Madam, yond fellow swears he will speak with you. **He's fortified against any denial**.

He's fortified against any denial – He won't take no for an answer

12

What kind o' man is he?

Why, of mankind.

What manner of man?

Of very ill manner; he'll speak with you, will you or no?

Of what personage and years is he?

Not yet old enough for a man, nor young enough for a boy.

Let him approach.

Give me my veil. We'll once more hear Orsino's embassy.

Olivia: Now, sir, what is your text?

Viola: Most sweet lady –

Olivia: A comfortable doctrine, and much may be said of it. Where lies your text?

Viola: In Orsino's bosom.

Olivia: In his bosom! In what chapter of his bosom?

Viola: To answer by the method, in the first of his heart.

Cesario (Viola) tries to tell Olivia how much Orsino loves her, but she won't listen.

Olivia: O, I have read it, it is heresy. Have you no more to say?

Viola: Good madam, let me see your face.

Olivia: Have you any commission from your lord to negotiate with my face? You are now out of your text, but **we will draw the curtain and show you the picture**. [*Unveiling*] Look you, sir, such a one I was this present. Is't not well done?

Olivia takes off her veil and pretends that her face is really a painting.

Viola: Excellently done – if God did all.

Olivia: 'Tis in grain, sir,'twill endure wind and weather.

Viola: 'Tis beauty truly blent, whose red and white
Nature's own sweet and cunning hand laid on.
Lady, you are the cruell'st she alive,
If you will lead these graces to the grave,
And leave the world no copy.

Olivia: O sir, I will not be so hard-hearted. I will give out divers schedules of my beauty. It shall be inventoried, and every particle and utensil labelled to my will. As, item: two lips, indifferent red; item: two grey eyes, with lids to them; item: one neck, one chin, and so forth. Were you sent hither to praise me?

Viola: I see you what you are, you are too proud.
But if you were the devil, you are fair.
My lord and master loves you.

Olivia: How does he love me?

Viola: With adorations, fertile tears,
With groans that thunder love, with sighs of fire.

Olivia: Your lord does know my mind, I cannot love him.
Yet I suppose him virtuous, know him noble,
Of great estate, of fresh and stainless youth,
In voices well divulg'd, free, learned, and valiant,
And in dimension and the shape of nature
A gracious person. But yet I cannot love him.
He might have took his answer long ago.

Viola: If I did love you in my master's flame,
With such a suffering, such a deadly life,
In your denial I would find no sense;
I would not understand it.

Olivia: Why, what would you?

Viola: Make me a willow cabin at your gate,
And call upon my soul within the house;
Write loyal **cantons** of contemned love,
And sing them loud even in the dead of night;
Halloo your name to the reverberate hills
And make the babbling gossip of the air
Cry out 'Olivia!' O, you should not rest
Between the elements of air and earth,
But you should pity me.

> **Think about it**
>
> What clues are there that Orsino might just have fallen in love with Olivia's looks?
>
> What do you learn about Orsino's character?
>
> Can you spot where Cesario (Viola) gives away his/her feelings to Orsino?

People say good things about him.

cantons – songs

| Act 1 Scene 5 | Olivia refuses to love Orsino, but she has fallen in love with Cesario (Viola). When Cesario leaves, Olivia sends Malvolio after him. |

peevish – cross/angry

Act 2 Scene 1	Sebastian, Viola's twin brother, has been saved by Antonio. He thinks Viola has been drowned.

Sebastian doesn't want Antonio to have bad luck by being with him.

Antonio: Will you stay no longer? Nor will you not that I go with you?

Sebastian: By your patience, no. **My stars shine darkly over me. The malignancy of my fate might perhaps distemper yours; therefore I shall crave of you your leave that I may bear my evils alone**.

Antonio: Let me yet know of you whither you are bound.

Sebastian: No, sooth, sir, **my determinate voyage is mere extravagancy**. My name is Sebastian. My father was that Sebastian of Messaline whom I know you have heard of. He left behind him myself and a sister, both born in an hour – if the heavens had been pleased, would we had so ended! But you, sir, altered that, for some hour before you took me from the breach of the sea was my sister drowned.

Sebastian doesn't have a plan.

Antonio: Alas the day!

Sebastian: A lady, sir, though it was said she much resembled me, was yet of many accounted beautiful.

Antonio: Let me be your servant.

Sebastian: If you will not undo what you have done – that is, kill him whom you have recovered – desire it not. I am bound to the Count Orsino's court. Farewell. [*Exit*]

Antonio: I have many enemies in Orsino's court,
Else would I very shortly see thee there –
But come what may, I do adore thee so
That danger shall seem sport, and I will go!

Think about it

What does this scene tell you about the love you can have for friends? What do you think of these two men?

Sebastian tells Antonio that his sister has drowned, but why doesn't this matter to us in the audience?

What is worrying about what Antonio says at the end?

Act 2 Scene 2	When Malvolio gives Cesario (Viola) the ring Viola knows that she didn't leave anything with Olivia. She knows now that Olivia has fallen in love with her as Cesario. She can only feel sorry.

Viola: I left no ring with her; what means this lady?
Fortune forbid my outside have not charm'd her!
She made good view of me, indeed so much
That – methought – her eyes had lost her tongue,
For she did speak in starts, distractedly.
She loves me, sure, the cunning of her passion
Invites me in this churlish messenger.
None of my lord's ring? Why, he sent her none.
I am the man! If it be so – as 'tis –
Poor lady, she were better love a dream.
Disguise, I see thou art a wickedness
Wherein the pregnant enemy does much.
How easy is it for the proper false
In women's waxen hearts to set their forms!
Alas, our frailty is the cause, not we,
For such as we are made, if such we be.
How will this **fadge**? My master loves her dearly;
And I, poor monster, fond as much on him;
And she, mistaken, seems to dote on me.
What will become of this? As I am man,
My state is desperate for my master's love.
As I am woman (now, alas the day!)
What thriftless sighs shall poor Olivia breathe?
O time, thou must untangle this, not I,
It is too hard a knot for me t' untie.

It's easy for women to fall for good looks.

fadge – turn out

Think about it

How does Viola work out that Olivia has fallen in love with her?
(It isn't just the ring!)

Can you find the line that tells you that Viola is in love with Orsino?

What kind of mess are they all in now?

Sir Toby and Sir Andrew are drunk. It is late and they are making a row. Olivia sends Malvolio to ask them to be quiet. He is rude and this annoys them.

My masters, are you mad? Or what are you? Is there no respect of place, persons, nor time in you?

My lady bade me tell you if you can separate yourself and your misdemeanors, you are welcome to the house. If not, she is very willing to bid you farewell.

Art any more than a steward? Dost thou think because thou art virtuous, there shall be **no more cakes and ale**?

For this **uncivil rule**, she shall know of it.

Go, shake your ears.

'Twere as good a deed as to drink when a man's a-hungry, to **challenge him the field** and then to break promise with him and make a fool of him.

no more cakes and ale – no more fun
challenge him the field – challenge him to a duel

uncivil rule – rude behaviour

Do 't, knight, I'll write thee a challenge; or I'll deliver thy indignation to him by word of mouth.

Sweet Sir Toby, be patient for tonight.

I will drop in his way some **obscure epistles** of love; I can write very like my lady, your niece.

He shall think by the letters that thou wilt drop that they come from my niece, and that she's in love with him.

My purpose is indeed a horse of that colour.

And your horse now would make him an ass.

Farewell.

She's a beagle and one that adores me.

I was adored once, too.

Come, come, I'll go **burn some sack**, 'tis too late to go to bed now. Come, knight.

obscure epistles – mysterious letters
burn some sack – warm up some sherry

| Act 2 Scene 4 | Orsino and Cesario (Viola) talk about love and what type of woman men should marry. |

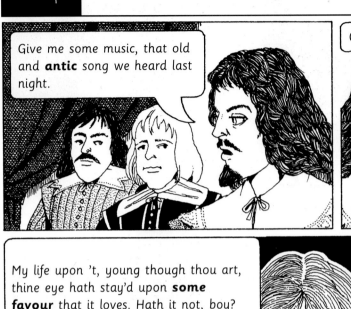

Give me some music, that old and **antic** song we heard last night.

Come hither, boy.

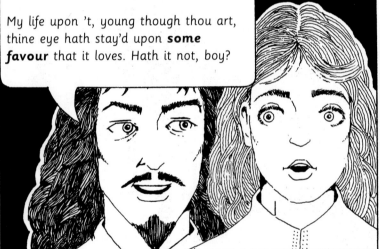

My life upon 't, young though thou art, thine eye hath stay'd upon **some favour** that it loves. Hath it not, boy?

What kind of woman is't?

Of your complexion.

She's not worth thee then. What years, i'faith?

About your years, my lord.

Too old by heaven!

antic – old fashioned
some favour – somebody

21

Let still the woman take an elder than herself, so wears she to him, **so sways she level** in her husband's heart.

For boy, however we do praise ourselves, our fancies are more giddy and unfirm, more longing, wavering, sooner lost and worn than women's are.

I think it well, my lord.

Then let thy love be younger than thyself, or thy affection **cannot hold the bent**.

For women are as roses, whose fair flower
Being once display'd, doth fall that very hour.

so sways she level – she is a good influence
I think it well – I agree
cannot hold the bent – cannot stand the strain

Orsino sends Cesario (Viola) off to
see Olivia once again.

Orsino: Once more, Cesario,
Get thee to yond same sovereign cruelty.
Tell her my love.

Viola: But if she cannot love you, sir?

Orsino: I cannot be so answer'd.

Viola: Sooth, but you must.
Say that some lady, as perhaps there is,
Hath for your love as great a pang of heart
As you have for Olivia: you cannot love her:
You tell her so. Must she not then be answer'd?

Orsino: There is no woman's sides
Can bide the beating of so strong a passion
As love doth give my heart; no woman's heart
So big, to hold so much: they lack retention.
**Alas, their love may be call'd appetite,
No motion of the liver, but the palate,
That suffers surfeit, cloyment, and revolt;**
But mine is all as hungry as the sea,
And can digest as much. Make no compare
Between that love a woman can bear me
And that I owe Olivia.

Women's love is like eating too
much food – you get sick of it.

Viola: Ay, but I know –

Orsino: What dost thou know?

Viola: Too well what love women to men may owe.
In faith, they are as true of heart as we.
My father had a daughter lov'd a man,
As it might be perhaps, were I a woman,
I should your lordship.

Orsino: And what's her history?

Viola: A blank, my lord: she never told her love,
But let concealment like a worm i'th' bud
Feed on her damask cheek: she pin'd in thought,
And with a green and yellow melancholy
She sat like Patience on a monument,
Smiling at grief. Was not this love indeed?
We men may say more, swear more, but indeed
Our shows are more than will: for still we prove
Much in our vows, but little in our love.

Orsino: But died thy sister of her love, my boy?

Viola: I am all the daughters of my father's house,
And all the brothers too; and yet I know not …
Sir, shall I to this lady?

Because she didn't tell anyone
about her love she became ill.
(damask = red, so her cheeks lost
their redness).

Think about it

Why do you feel sorry for Viola in this scene?

Do you agree with what Orsino says about the differences between a man's and a woman's love?

Can you find the lines where Viola almost gives away her love for Orsino?

What sad thing is Viola thinking of when she says that she is 'all the brothers too'? (We, of course, know that she has no reason to be sad.)

All of this scene shows us **dramatic irony**, because Viola is speaking about herself but she can't say so and Orsino doesn't know it.

Act 2 Scene 5	Sir Toby, Sir Andrew, Maria and Fabian wait for Malvolio to find the forged letter. Malvolio is day-dreaming about being married to Olivia.

Get ye all three into the box tree. Malvolio's coming down this walk.

Maria once told me she did **affect** me, and I have heard herself come thus near . . .

. . . that should she fancy, it should be one of my complexion.

Here's an overweening rogue.

'Slight. I could so beat the rogue.

To be Count Malvolio!

Calling my officers about me, having come from a day-bed, where I have left Olivia sleeping.

And then **to have humour of state**: and **after a demure travel of regard**, telling them I know my place, as I would they should theirs, to ask for my kinsman, Toby.

Bolts and shackles!

affect – admire
to have humour of state – to enjoy my new power
after a demure travel of regard – after inspecting them

Malvolio imagines being able to tell
Sir Toby to behave himself. Sir Toby
is furious.

Malvolio: Toby approaches; curtsies there to me –

Sir Toby: Shall this fellow live?

**Fabian: Though our silence be drawn from us with
cars, yet peace!**

Fabian tells the others to keep
quiet, but only the audience can
hear what they say – Malvolio can't.

Malvolio will give Sir Toby a mean
look.

Malvolio: I extend my hand to him thus, **quenching
my familiar smile with an austere regard of control** –

Sir Toby: And does not Toby take you a blow o' the
lips then?

Malvolio: Saying, 'Cousin Toby, my fortunes having
cast me on your niece give me this prerogative of speech'

Sir Toby: What, what?

Malvolio: 'You must amend your drunkenness.'

Sir Toby: Out, scab!

Fabian: Nay, patience, or we break the sinews of our plot.

Malvolio: 'Besides, you waste the treasure of your
time with a foolish knight' –

Sir Andrew: That's me, I warrant you.

Malvolio: 'One Sir Andrew.'

Sir Andrew: I knew 'twas I, for many do call me fool.

Think about it

What does this tell
you about Malvolio's
character?

Why do you think
this scene looks
funny on the stage?

What do the
audience know that
Malvolio doesn't?

Malvolio reads the forged letter. He believes that Olivia really does love him.

What employment have we here?

By my life, this is my lady's hand. Her very phrases.

If this fall into thy hand, revolve. In my stars I am above thee, but be not afraid of greatness. Some are born great, some achieve greatness, and some have greatness thrust on 'em......

...Remember who commended thy yellow stockings, and wished to see thee ever cross-gartered.

I thank my stars. I am happy. I will be strange, stout, in yellow stockings and cross-gartered.

Here is yet a postscript.

I will smile, I will do everything that thou wilt have me.

If thou entertain'st my love, let it appear in thy smiling. Therefore in my presence still smile, dear my sweet, I prithee.

Cesario (Viola) returns to Olivia's house. He jokes with the Clown before the Clown goes to fetch Olivia.

Save thee, friend, and thy music. Dost thou live by the **tabor**?

No sir, I live by the church.

Art thou a churchman?

No such matter, sir, I do live by the church, for I do live at my house, and my house doth stand by the church.

So thou may'st say the king lies by a beggar, if a beggar dwell near him; or the church stands by thy tabor, if thy tabor stand by the church.

My lady is within, sir. I will **conster** to them whence you come.

tabor – drum
conster – tell

<table>
<tr><td>

**Act 3
Scene 1**

</td><td>

Olivia tells Cesario (Viola) that she
loves him. Cesario pities her and says
he can never love any woman.

</td></tr>
</table>

Olivia: Give me leave, I beseech you. I did send,
After the last enchantment you did here,
A ring in chase of you. So did I abuse
Myself, my servant, and, I fear me, you.
Under your hard construction must I sit,
To force that on you in a shameful cunning
Which you knew none of yours. **What might you think?**
Have you not set mine honour at the stake,
And baited it with all th'unmuzzled thoughts
That tyrannous heart can think? To one of your receiving
Enough is shown; a **cypress**, not a bosom,
Hides my heart. So, let me hear you speak.

Olivia asks Cesario (Viola) what he
must think of her, now that she has
told him that she loves him.

cypress – thin material

Viola: I pity you.

Olivia: That's a degree to love.

Viola: No, not a grize; for 'tis **a vulgar proof**
That very oft we pity enemies.

a vulgar proof – often the case

Olivia: Why then methinks 'tis time to smile again.
O world, how apt the poor are to be proud!
If one should be a prey, how much the better
To fall before the lion than the wolf! [*A clock strikes*]
The clock upbraids me with the waste of time.
Be not afraid, good youth, I will not have you,
And yet when wit and youth is come to harvest,
Your wife is like to reap a proper man.
There lies your way, due west.

Viola: Then westward ho!
Grace and good disposition attend your ladyship!
You'll nothing, madam, to my lord, by me?

Olivia: Stay.
I prithee, tell me what thou think'st of me.

Viola: That you do think you are not what you are.

Olivia: If I think so, I think the same of you.

Viola: Then think you right; I am not what I am.

There is a play on words here because Cesario (Viola) is not what he seems and Olivia doesn't know what Cesario is!

Olivia: I would you were as I would have you be.

Viola: Would it be better, madam, than I am?
I wish it might, for now I am your fool.

Olivia: Cesario, by the roses of the spring,
By maidenhood, honour, truth, and everything,
I love thee so, that maugre all thy pride,
Nor wit nor reason can my passion hide.
Do not extort thy reasons from this clause,
For that I woo, thou therefore hast no cause;
But rather reason thus with reason fetter:
Love sought, is good; but given unsought, is better.

Viola: By innocence I swear, and by my youth,
I have one heart, one bosom, and one truth.
And that no woman has, nor never none
Shall mistress be of it, save I alone.
And so adieu, good madam; never more
Will I my master's tears to you deplore.

Olivia: Yet come again; for thou perhaps may'st move
That heart, which now abhors, to like his love.

Think about it

How do you feel about Olivia, now that she has revealed her love for Cesario (Viola)?

What must Viola be thinking now?

We still can't be too sad because this is a comedy – so what might happen that will make things turn out well?

Sir Toby and Fabian tease Sir Andrew. They say he should challenge Cesario (Viola) to a duel to impress Olivia. Maria arrives with news of Malvolio.

Marry, I saw your niece do more favours to the Count's serving-man than ever she bestowed upon me.

Did she see thee the while, old boy, tell me that?

As plain as I see you now.

This was a great argument of love in her toward you.

'Slight! Will you make an ass o' me?

She did show favour to the youth in your sight only to exasperate you, to awake your dormouse valour, to put fire in your heart, and brimstone in your liver.

Challenge me the Count's youth to fight with him; hurt him in eleven places; my niece shall take note of it.

We shall have a rare letter from him.

I think oxen and **wainropes** cannot hale them together.

For Andrew, if he were opened and you find so much blood in his liver as will clog the foot of a flea, I'll eat the rest of th' anatomy.

And his opposite, the youth, bears in his **visage** no great **presage** of cruelty.

If you desire the spleen and laugh yourselves into stitches, follow me.

He's in yellow stockings!

And cross-gartered?

Most villainously. You have not seen such a thing as 'tis.

wainropes – thick ropes for pulling carts
visage – face

presage – sign
Most villainously – He looks awful!

Sebastian and Antonio arrive. Antonio once fought against Orsino. He does not feel safe in the city. He lends Sebastian his purse and goes to book rooms.

I could not stay behind you ... what might befall your travel, **being skilless** in these parts.

Thanks and ever thanks.

What's to do? Shall we go see the **relics** of this town?

Tomorrow, sir, best first go see your lodging.

Let us satisfy our eyes with the memorials and the things of fame that do renown this city.

I do not without danger walk these streets. Once in a seafight 'gainst the Count I did some service.

Do not then walk too open.

Hold, sir, here's my purse. In the south suburbs is best to lodge.

being skilless – being a stranger
relics – historical sights

Malvolio is dressed to impress! He has followed all the instructions in the forged letter. Olivia is *not* impressed!

Good Maria, let this fellow be looked to. Where's my cousin Toby? Let some of my people have a special care of him.

This **concurs** directly with the letter. She sends him on purpose, that I may appear stubborn to him.

Which way is he, in the name of sanctity?

Go off I discard you. Let me enjoy my **private**. Go off.

How do you, Malvolio? How is't with you?

Go hang yourselves all: you are idle, shallow things, **I am not of your element**.

Come, we'll have him in a dark room and bound. My niece is already in the belief that he's mad.

We may carry it thus for our pleasure and his penance.

concurs – agrees **private** – privacy
I am not of your element – I am better than you

36

Sir Andrew has written the letter challenging Cesario (Viola) to a duel. Sir Toby reads it and thinks of a better way to make Cesario fight.

Here's the challenge, read it.
I warrant there's vinegar and pepper in't.

If this letter move him not, his legs cannot. I'll give't him.

You may have very fit occasion for't: he is now in some **commerce** with my lady and will by and by depart.

Go, Sir Andrew, scout me for him.

Now will I not deliver his letter.

This letter, being so excellently ignorant, will breed no terror in the youth: he will find it comes from a clodpole.

I will deliver his challenge by word of mouth, set upon Aguecheek a notable report of valour, and drive the gentleman into a most hideous opinion of his rage, skill, fury and impetuosity.

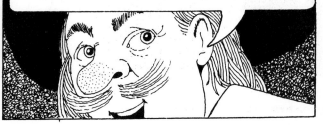

commerce – business
scout me for him – find him

Here he comes with your niece: **give them way** till he take leave and presently after him.

I will mediate the while upon some horrid message for a challenge.

I have said too much unto a heart of stone.

What will you ask of me that I'll deny?

Nothing but this, your true love for my master.

How with mine honour may I give him that Which I have given to you?

I will acquit you.

Well, come again tomorrow. Fare thee well.

give them way – leave them

<table>
<tr><td>

**Act 3
Scene 4**

</td><td>

Sir Toby continues to have fun. Now he tells Cesario (Viola) how brave and fierce Sir Andrew is.

</td></tr>
</table>

Sir Toby: Of what nature the wrongs are thou hast done him, I know not: but thy intercepter, full of despite, bloody as the hunter, attends thee at the orchard end. **Dismount thy tuck**, be yare in thy preparation, for thy assailant is quick, skilful, and deadly.

Dismount thy tuck – draw your sword

Viola: You mistake, sir; I am sure no man hath any quarrel to me. My remembrance is very free and clear from any image of offence done to any man.

Sir Toby: You'll find it otherwise, I assure you. Therefore, if you hold your life at any price, betake you to your guard: for **your opposite hath in him what youth, strength, skill, and wrath, can furnish man withal.**

Sir Toby is describing Sir Andrew to Cesario (Viola) and of course lying about how good a fighter he is.

Viola: I pray you, sir, what is he?

Sir Toby: He is knight, **dubbed with unhatched rapier, and on carpet consideration**, but he is a devil in a private brawl. Souls and bodies hath he divorced three, and his incensement at this moment is so implacable that satisfaction can be none but by pangs of death and **sepulchre**. Hob, nob is his word: give't or take't.

Sir Andrew wasn't knighted for bravery in battle.

sepulchre – a tomb where someone is buried

Viola: I will return again into the house, and desire some conduct of the lady. I am no fighter. **I have heard of some kind of men that put quarrels purposely on others to taste their valour: belike this is a man of that quirk.**

Cesario (Viola) is right about the kind of man Sir Toby is but doesn't know it. This is called **dramatic irony**.

Sir Toby: Sir, no: his indignation derives itself out of a very competent injury: therefore get you on, and give him his desire. Back you shall not to the house, unless you undertake that with me which with as much safety you might answer him; therefore on, or strip your sword stark naked: for meddle you must, that's certain, **or forswear to wear iron about you.**

Sir Toby says that unless Cesario (Viola) comes prepared to fight, he'll think him a coward.

Viola: This is as uncivil as strange. I beseech you, do me this courteous office, as to know of the knight what my offence to him is: it is something of my negligence, nothing of my purpose.

Sir Toby: I will do so. Signior Fabian, stay you by this gentleman till my return. [*Exit Sir Toby*]

Viola: Pray you, sir, do you know of this matter?

Fabian: I know the knight is incensed against you, even to a mortal arbitrement, but nothing of the circumstance more.

Viola: I beseech you, what manner of man is he?

Fabian: Nothing of that wonderful promise, to read him by his form, as you are like to find him in the proof of his valour. He is indeed, sir, the most skilful, bloody, and fatal opposite that you could possibly have found in any part of Illyria. Will you walk towards him, I will make your peace with him if I can.

Viola: I shall be much bound to you for't. I am one that had rather go with Sir Priest than Sir Knight: I care not who knows so much of my mettle.

Think about it

Sir Toby is supposed to be a comical person, but do you think there is anything mean about him here?

We know that Viola is disguised as the man Cesario, so what are we wondering will happen now?

Then Sir Toby tells Sir Andrew the same sort of things about Cesario (Viola)!

Why man, he's a very devil. They say he has been fencer to the **Sophy**.

I'll not meddle with him.

Ay, but he will not now be pacified.

Plague on't, and I thought he had been valiant and so cunning in fence, I'd have seen him damned ere I'd have challenged him.

Let him let the matter slip, and I'll give him my horse.

Come, Sir Andrew, there's no remedy, the gentleman will for his honour's sake have one bout with you.

I do assure you, 'tis against my will.

Sophy – Shah (ruler) of Persia

Antonio arrives. He thinks that Cesario (Viola) is Sebastian and stops the duel. Orsino's officers come and arrest Antonio. He asks for his purse back.

Put up your sword! If this young gentleman have done offence, I take the fault on me.

Pray sir, put your sword up, if you please.

Marry, will I, sir.

Antonio . . .

. . . I arrest thee at the suit of Count Orsino.

This comes with seeking you.

I must entreat of you some of that money.

What money, sir?

For the fair kindness you have show'd me here, I'll lend you something.

| Act 3 Scene 4 | Antonio is really upset with who he thinks is Sebastian. Of course, Viola (Cesario) does not know what he is talking about, but she does hear something that gives her hope. |

Antonio: Will you deny me now?
Is't possible that my deserts to you
Can lack persuasion? Do not tempt my misery,
Lest that it make me so unsound a man
As to upbraid you with those kindnesses
That I have done for you.

Antonio doesn't want to appear mean by reminding Sebastian of all the favours he's done him.

Viola: I know of none,
Nor know I you by voice or any feature.
I hate ingratitude more in a man
Than lying, vainness, babbling drunkenness,
Or any taint of vice whose strong corruption
Inhabits our frail blood.

Antonio: O heavens themselves!

Officer: Come sir, I pray you go.

Antonio: Let me speak a little. This youth that you see here
I snatch'd one half out of the jaws of death,
Reliev'd him with such sanctity of love;
And to his image, which methought did promise
Most venerable worth, did I devotion.

Officer: What's that to us? The time goes by. Away!

Antonio: But O how vile an idol proves this god!
Thou hast, Sebastian, done good feature shame.
In nature there's no blemish but the mind.
None can be call'd deform'd but the unkind.
Virtue is beauty, but the beauteous evil
Are empty trunks, o'er-flourish'd by the devil.

Officer: The man grows mad, away with him. Come, come, sir.

Antonio: Lead me on. *Exit [with officers]*

43

Viola: Methinks his words do from such passion fly
That he believes himself; so do not I:
Prove true, imagination, O prove true –
That I, dear brother, be now ta'en for you!

He nam'd Sebastian. I my brother know
Yet living in my glass. Even such and so
In favour was my brother, and he went
Still in this fashion, colour, ornament,
For him I imitate. O, if it prove,
Tempests are kind, and salt waves fresh in love! [*Exit*]

Sir Toby: A very dishonest paltry boy, and more a
coward than a hare.

Fabian: A coward, a most devout coward, religious
in it.

Sir Andrew: 'Slid, I'll after him again, and beat him.

'Slid – 'by God's eyelid'

Sir Toby: Do, cuff him soundly, but never draw thy
sword.

Think about it

What has Antonio done to make you think that
he really is a good friend to Sebastian?

How do you think Antonio feels now?

Remember that this is a comedy – why are we
not too worried about Antonio and Viola at this
point?

45

Come, sir, I will not let you go. Put up your **iron**. Come on!

I will be free from thee. What woulds't thou now?

If thou dar'st tempt me further, draw thy sword.

What, what! Nay, then, I must have an ounce or two of this **malapert** blood from you.

Hold, Toby!

Be not offended, dear Cesario.

Go with me to my house, and hear thou there how many fruitless pranks this ruffian hath **botch'd up**.

What relish is in this? How runs the stream? Or I am mad, or else this is a dream.

iron – sword
botch'd up – messed up

malapert – cheeky

46

Malvolio has been locked in a dark room. The Clown pretends to be a curate (priest) to make more fun of him.

Put on this gown, and this beard, make him believe thou art Sir Topas the curate.

What ho, I say. Peace in this prison.

Who calls there?

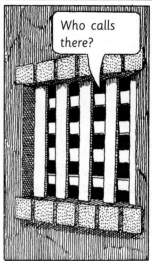

Sir Topas the curate, who comes to visit Malvolio the lunatic.

Sir Topas, Sir Topas, good Sir Topas, go to my lady.

Out hyperbolical fiend! how vexest thou this man! Talkest thou nothing but of ladies?

Sir Topas, never was man thus wronged.

Good Sir Topas, do not think I am mad.

They have laid me here in hideous darkness.

Out hyperbolical fiend! The Clown pretends to speak to a devil that has taken over Malvolio's mind.

Then the Clown speaks in his own voice.

Alas, sir, **how fell you besides your five wits?**

Fool, there was never man so notoriously abused.

I am as well in my wits, fool as thou art.

Then you are mad indeed, if you be no better in your wits than a fool.

Good fool, help me to some light and some paper: I tell thee I am as well in my wits as any man in Illyria.

Well-a-day that you were, sir!

By this hand, I am! Good fool, some ink, paper, and light and convey what I will set down to my lady.

how fell you besides your five wits? – how did you lose your senses?

48

Act 4 Scene 3	Sebastian thinks that after all that's happened to him, everyone must be crazy! He wonders where Antonio is. Olivia arrives and asks him to marry her. They go off with the priest to get married.

Sebastian: This is the air, that is the glorious sun,
This pearl she gave me, I do feel't, and see't,
And though 'tis wonder that enwraps me thus,
Yet 'tis not madness. Where's Antonio then?
I could not find him at **the Elephant**,
Yet there he was, and there I found this credit,
That he did range the town to seek me out.
His counsel now might do me golden service:
For though my soul disputes well with my sense
That this may be some error, but no madness,
Yet doth this accident and flood of fortune
So far exceed all instance, all discourse,
That I am ready to distrust mine eyes,
And wrangle with my reason that persuades me
To any other trust but that I am mad,
Or else the lady's mad; yet if 'twere so,
She could not sway her house, command her followers,
Take and give back affairs and their dispatch,
With such a smooth, discreet, and stable bearing
As I perceive she does. There's something in't
That is deceivable. But here the lady comes.

the Elephant – an inn

Sebastian decides that what's happening can't be so bad, because Olivia seems to be a good woman, in charge of servants and a house.

[*Enter* Olivia *and a priest*]

Olivia: Blame not this haste of mine. If you mean well,
Now go with me, and with this holy man,
Into the chantry by; there before him,
And underneath that consecrated roof,
Plight me the full assurance of your faith,
That my most jealous and too doubtful soul
May live at peace. **He shall conceal it,**
Whiles you are willing it shall come to note,
What time we will our celebration keep
According to my birth. What do you say?

Olivia asks Sebastian to marry her.

Olivia is willing to keep the marriage secret until Sebastian wants people to know.

Sebastian: I'll follow this good man, and go with you,
And having sworn truth, ever will be true.

Olivia: Then lead the way, good father, and heavens
so shine,
That they may fairly note this act of mine!

Think about it

Before the last act, let's remind ourselves what the different characters believe at this point.

Which characters are having these thoughts at the moment?

My brother might be alive.

They're all crazy round here!

My sister is dead.

I wish I could tell Orsino that I love him.

I've just married Cesario.

I wonder where Antonio is.

What went wrong? I did everything she said in the letter.

I wonder why Olivia won't marry me.

Why is Sebastian pretending he doesn't know me?

What do you think of Sebastian marrying Olivia so quickly?

What do you think will happen when they all meet up?

Act 5 Scene 1	Antonio is brought before Orsino. He sees Cesario (Viola) but thinks he/she is Sebastian.

Here comes the man, sir, that did rescue me.

That face of his I do remember well; yet when I saw it last, it was besmear'd as black as **Vulcan**, in the smoke of war.

He did me kindness, sir, **drew** on my side.

Notable pirate, thou salt-water thief, what foolish boldness brought thee to thine enemies?

Orsino, noble sir, be pleas'd that I shake off these names you give me.

That most ungrateful boy there by your side, from the rude sea's enrag'd and foamy mouth did I **redeem**.

For his sake did I expose myself into the danger of this town.

How can this be?

Here comes the Countess.

Vulcan – the Roman god of fire and blacksmiths.
drew – (his sword)   **redeem** – rescue

51

<table>
<tr>
<td>

**Act 5
Scene 1**

</td>
<td>

Orsino is really cross with Olivia because she cannot love him. Olivia is cross with Cesario (Viola) because she thinks he/she is Sebastian, her husband, and should not be at Orsino's house. She tells them about her marriage.

</td>
<td>

</td>
</tr>
</table>

Orsino: Still so cruel?

Olivia: Still so constant, lord.

Orsino: What, to perverseness? **You uncivil lady,
To whose ingrate and unauspicious altars
My soul the faithfull'st off'rings hath breath'd out
That e'er devotion tender'd** – What shall I do?

Orsino tells Olivia how ungrateful she is.

Olivia: Even what it please my lord that shall become him.

Orsino: Why should I not, had I the heart to do it,
Like to th'Egyptian thief at point of death,
Kill what I love? a savage jealousy
That sometimes savours nobly. But hear me this:
Since you to non-regardance cast my faith,
And that I partly know the instrument
That screws me from my true place in your favour,
Live you the marble-breasted tyrant still.
But this your minion, whom I know you love,
And whom, by heaven, I swear I tender dearly,
Him will I tear out of that cruel eye
Where he sits crowned in his master's spite.
Come, boy, with me; my thoughts are ripe in mischief:
**I'll sacrifice the lamb that I do love,
To spite a raven's heart within a dove.**

Orsino is jealous and says that he will kill Cesario (Viola), even though he loves him, just because Cesario is loved by Olivia.

Viola: And I most jocund, apt, and willingly,
To do you rest, a thousand deaths would die.

Olivia: Where goes Cesario?

Viola: After him I love
More than I love these eyes, more than my life,
More, by all mores, than e'er I shall love wife.
If I do feign, you witnesses above
Punish my life, for tainting of my love.

Olivia: Ay me detested! How am I **beguil'd**!

Viola: Who does beguile you? Who does do you wrong?

Olivia: Hast thou forgot thyself? Is it so long?
[*To a servant*] Call forth the holy father.

Orsino: Come, away!

Olivia: Whither, my lord? Cesario, husband, stay!

Orsino: Husband?

Olivia: Ay, husband. Can he that deny?

Orsino: Her husband, sirrah?

Viola: No, my lord, not I.

Olivia: Alas, it is the baseness of thy fear
That makes thee strangle thy propriety.
Fear not, Cesario, take thy fortunes up.
Be that thou know'st thou art, and then thou art
As great as that thou fear'st.
                    [*Enter the priest*]
O welcome, father!
Father, I charge thee by thy reverence
Here to unfold what thou dost know
Hath newly pass'd between this youth and me.

Priest: A contract of eternal bond of love.

Cesario (Viola) declares his/her love for Orsino.

beguiled – cheated

Think about it

Why does Orsino think that Olivia is cruel?

Do you feel sorry for Olivia at this point?

Why can we laugh when Cesario (Viola) says, 'No, my lord, not I'?

We know that things will turn out fine – so what are we waiting for now?

| Act 5 Scene 1 | Sir Andrew and Sir Toby come in injured. Sebastian has really hurt them! |

For the love of God, a surgeon!

What's the matter?

He has broken my head across, and has given Sir Toby a bloody coxcomb too.

Who has done this, Sir Andrew?

The Count's gentleman, one Cesario. We took him for a coward but he's the very devil.

My gentleman, Cesario?

Why do you speak to me? I never hurt you. You drew your sword upon me without cause, but I hurt you not.

I'll help you, Sir Toby.

Will you help? An asshead, a thin-faced knave, a gull.

Get him to bed, and let his hurt be looked to.

coxcomb – head
gull – fool

Sebastian arrives, having hit Sir Toby. Cesario (Viola) and Sebastian are on stage together and everyone finds out that they are twins. Everybody is happy. They send for Malvolio.

Sebastian: I am sorry, madam, I have hurt your kinsman.
But had it been the brother of my blood,
I must have done no less, with wit and safety.
**You throw a strange regard upon me; and by that
I do perceive it hath offended you:**
Pardon me, sweet one, even for the vows
We made each other but so late ago.

Olivia's face isn't strange because she is cross, but because she can't believe her eyes.

Orsino: One face, one voice, one habit, and two persons!
A natural perspective, that is, and is not!

Sebastian: Antonio! My dear Antonio,
How have the hours rack'd and tortur'd me,
Since I have lost thee!

Antonio: Sebastian are you?

Sebastian: Fear'st thou that, Antonio?

Antonio: How have you made division of yourself?
An apple cleft in two is not more twin
Than these two creatures. Which is Sebastian?

Olivia: Most wonderful!

Sebastian: Do I stand there? I never had a brother;
Nor can there be that deity in my nature
Of here and everywhere. I had a sister,
Whom the blind waves and surges have devour'd:
Of charity, what kin are you to me?
What countryman? What name? What parentage?

Viola: Of Messaline: Sebastian was my father;
Such a Sebastian was my brother too:
So went he suited to his **watery tomb**.
If spirits can assume both form and suit,
You come to fright us.

watery tomb – drowned

Cesario (Viola) thinks that
Sebastian could be a ghost or a
spirit.

Sebastian: A spirit I am indeed,
But am in that dimension grossly clad
Which from the womb I did participate.
Were you a woman, as the rest goes even,
I should my tears let fall upon your cheek,
And say, 'Thrice welcome, drowned Viola.'

Viola: I am Viola; which to confirm,
I'll bring you to a captain in this town,
Where lie my **maiden weeds**; by whose gentle help
I was preserv'd to serve this noble count:
All the occurance of my fortune since
Hath been between this lady and this lord.

maiden weeds – women's clothes

Sebastian: [*To Olivia*] So comes it, lady, you have
been mistook.
But nature to her bias drew in that.
You would have been contracted to a maid;
Nor are you therein, by my life deceiv'd:
You are betrothed both to a maid and man.

Orsino: Be not amaz'd, right noble is his blood.
If this be so, as yet the glass seems true,
I shall have share in this most happy wreck.
[*To Viola*] Boy, thou hast said to me a thousand times
Thou never should'st love woman like to me.

Think about it

Why does Olivia look at
Sebastian strangely when he
first arrives?

Where would you place
the actors on the stage to
make the most of the
meeting between the twins?

Nobody talks about
Antonio, the prisoner.
What do you think will
happen to him?

**Viola: And all those swearings will I over-swear,
And all those swearings keep as true in soul
As doth that orbed continent the fire
That severs night from day.**

Viola declares her love for Orsino.

Orsino: Give me thy hand,
And let me see thee in thy woman's weeds.

Malvolio finds out that he has been tricked when he shows Olivia the forged letter. He storms off but Orsino sends Fabian after him to calm him down.

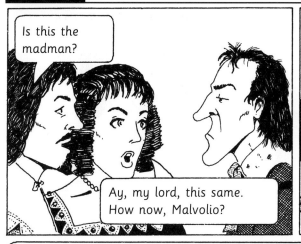

Is this the madman?

Ay, my lord, this same. How now, Malvolio?

Madam, you have done me wrong, notorious wrong.

Have I, Malvolio? No.

Lady, you have. Pray you, **peruse** that letter. You must not now deny it is your hand.

Alas, Malvolio, this is not my writing, though I confess much like the character: but, out of question, 'tis Maria's hand.

Most freely I confess, myself and Toby set this **device** against Malvolio.

Maria writ the letter, at Sir Toby's great **importance**, in **recompense** whereof he hath married her.

Alas, poor fool, how have they baffled thee!

peruse – read
device – trick

importance – encouragement
recompense – payment

I was one, sir, in this interlude, one Sir Topas, sir.

I'll be reveng'd on the whole pack of you!

He hath been most notoriously abused.

Pursue him, and entreat him to a peace.

Cesario, come; for so you shall be while you are a man; but when in other **habits** you are seen, Orsino's **mistress** and his **fancy**'s queen.

habits – clothes   **mistress** – wife
fancy's – love's

A great while ago the world begun,
With hey, ho, the wind and the rain,
But that's all one, our play is done,
And we'll strive to please you every day.

THE END